DISCARDED

IMAGES
of America

BURLINGTON

D1066662

IMAGES
of America

BURLINGTON

David Robinson and Mary Ann DiSpirito

ARCADIA

F
59
.B 9
R 65
1997

First published 1997
Copyright © David Robinson and Mary Ann DiSpirito, 1997

ISBN 0-7524-0456-3

Published by Arcadia Publishing,
an imprint of the Chalford Publishing Corporation,
One Washington Center, Dover, New Hampshire 03820.
Printed in Great Britain

Library of Congress Cataloging-in-Publication Data applied for

LIBRARY
BUNKER HILL COMMUNITY COLLEGE
CHARLESTOWN. MASS. 02129

COVER: City crews clear snow on Church Street after a blizzard, December 3, 1936.
Photograph by L.L. McAllister.

Contents

Acknowledgments

We are grateful to Louis DiSpirito for his help with research and general moral support, Felicia M. Robinson for her support and patience, historian Jerry Fox for assistance with captions and historical accuracy, and to the following contributors:

Bove's Restaurant-Richard Bove
The Burlington Department of Public Works, Water Division-Thomas M. Dion, CPO
The Gerald B. Fox Collection
The Ethan Allen Club
The Ethan Allen Homestead
The archives of Fletcher Allen Health Care, compliments of Public Relations Department
The Fletcher Free Library-Amber Collins, co-director
Sylvia Heininger Holden
The Alfred Holden Collection
The Lake Champlain Regional Chamber of Commerce
The Lake Champlain Transportation Co. for photographs of lake transportation
Rita Lefebvre
Jeanne Carter Miller
North Country Books, Burlington, VT—photographs of dignitaries courtesy of Mark Ciufo
   and Joel Dumas
Howard Porter
Mr. and Mrs. Walter W. Richard
The archives of the Roman Catholic Diocese of Burlington
Trinity College of Vermont/Sisters of Mercy
The Visiting Nurse Association

We also acknowledge our debt for information provided by Charles Allen's *About Burlington Vermont* (1905), from which some images were drawn; Arthur F. Stone's *Vermont of Today* (1929, 3 vols.); Lilian Baker Carlisle's, Margaret Muller's, David Blow's, and Samuel Hatfield's *Look Around Burlington, Vermont* (1972); Steven Roth's *History of Trinity College, 1925–1927* (1975); Peter Carlough's *Bygone Burlington* (1977); The Burlington Airport Commissioners' *Burlington International Airport: A Pictorial History* (1982); Wesley Abell's and Joseph Heald's *History of Ethan Allen Engine Company No. 4 of Burlington, Vermont and of the Ethan Allen Club, 1857–1982* (1982); Ralph Nading Hill's "Two Centuries of Ferry Boating on Lake Champlain," in *Lake Champlain Ferryboats* published by the Lake Champlain Transportation Co. (1990); David Blow's and Lilian Baker Carlisle's *Historic Guide to Burlington Neighborhoods* (1991); and Robert Michaud's *Salute to Burlington* (1991).

Introduction

Burlington, Vermont, is situated in Chittenden County on the eastern shore of Lake Champlain. Chartered by Benning Wentworth, the Colonial governor of New Hampshire on June 7, 1763, the original town contained 36 square miles. Township proprietors held their first meeting in Salisbury, Connecticut, in March of 1774, with Col. Thomas Chittenden as moderator and Ira Allen as clerk. Ethan Allen and Remember Baker were among the proprietors. A few logs lashed together as a makeshift wharf on the bay near the foot of King Street marked the beginning of commercial activity on the waterfront. In 1791, three houses were situated near the foot of Battery Street. When Prince Edward, Queen Victoria's father, visited during the winter of 1793, only seven houses existed in the village.

Burlington was organized in March 1797. By 1800, the population was steadily increasing, the wharves were being extended, and residences and businesses were spreading up the hillside. In 1865, the town was incorporated as a city, and the population rose to 14,387 in 1870.

The Burlington Board of Trade in 1889 wrote:

> Burlington is the metropolis of Vermont, the capital of Chittenden County, and the trade center of Lake Champlain. It stands on the old seigniory of La Manaudiere, the property of Pierre Ramibault when the French began to settle on Lake Champlain. . . . No city or village in New England surpasses Burlington in beauty of location. . . . Burlington is fortunate not only in natural location and surroundings, but is kept inviting and healthy. Its streets are well-lined with shade trees, the water supply is pure and abundant, the police force prompt and efficient in enforcing the laws, and the fire department thoroughly organized, and supplemented by the fire alarm telegraph and telephone, furnish protection to property.

These qualities have continued to attract visitors and new residents to Burlington for the one hundred and eight years since.

No book, especially a short one, can include all of the images of people and places that every reader might wish to see. Some photographs we sought were unavailable to us; some were selected for historical importance, even when the images were unclear because there were no other accessible depictions of that particular person or place. As the reader will notice from the photos that show empty streets, early photographers were careful to exclude people from their images, as the exposure times needed were so long that most human subjects blurred.

We have endeavored to provide an overview of Burlington from 1860 to 1960, a century of tremendous growth for this small city. Through the generosity and support of individuals and businesses with private collections, we have included many photographs in this book that have not been published within the last thirty-five years. Buildings long absent from the cityscape and many of the faces you will see here may be unfamiliar today, yet they were the Burlington known by generations past. These Burlingtonians helped to build their community and, in some cases, gave their services to the nation.

Compiling this book has given us a deeper sense of our own connection to the Burlington of years ago. We hope the reader will enjoy, in these images, that same connection.

David Robinson
Mary Ann DiSpirito
Burlington, Vermont
April 1997

One
Lakefront

Beginning in 1809, Champlain was the first lake in the world with regularly scheduled steamboat service. Ease of water travel and the advent of the railway system made Burlington a hub of commerce. The Central Vermont Railway terminal located at the foot of College Street and seen behind the pier was built during the Civil War.

In 1900, Burlington still depended upon railroad and lake transportation for its economic prosperity. Freight yards owned by the Central Vermont, Burlington & Lamoille, and Rutland & Burlington railroads handled most of the goods going in and out of Burlington.

The Lake Champlain Yacht Club was organized on May 16, 1887, and incorporated November 16, 1892. The original structure, shown around 1895, burned on November 15, 1901.

Waterfront Yacht Club Slip, Burlington, Vt.

In 1905, the Yacht Club had one hundred and thirty active members, who kept a fleet of thirty-one power yachts and twenty-nine sailing yachts moored in this slip. The club's annual regattas were a summer social event.

Burlington, Vt., Yacht Club and Harbor.

The rebuilt Yacht Club opened on May 26, 1903.

The government wanted the light tenders to live in a house built for them on the breakwater. Completed in December 1874, the dwelling was never occupied. The government sold it at auction in 1884, and the structure was moved to Blodgett Street, where it still stands. The Pioneer Shops can be seen in the foreground.

In the 1800s, lumber was one of Burlington's major products. Lawrence Barnes opened the first yard in 1856. Burlington in 1873 was the third largest lumber port in the country, behind Albany and Chicago. By 1889, five firms employed over one thousand men.

The Pioneer Shops were like today's incubator businesses. Congestion on the 1880s waterfront property reflects the need for manufacturers to be close to the water and rail transport.

In 1929, the lumberyards, docks, and Union Station were all major landmarks. Main Street is pictured in the center, with College Street on the left and King Street on the right. The residential area in the upper left was razed for urban renewal during the 1960s.

Union Station and King Street docks handled most of the passenger and freight travel into Burlington until the middle of this century. Follett House is located right of top center, and Pease Grain is located in the upper left corner.

By the time George N. Lathrop of Bristol took this aerial photograph, passenger travel by rail had diminished, although freight and lumber were still being brought in by train.

This is a photograph of Burlington before urban renewal. Much of the residential area left of center is now covered by hotels, apartments, commercial buildings, and shopping areas.

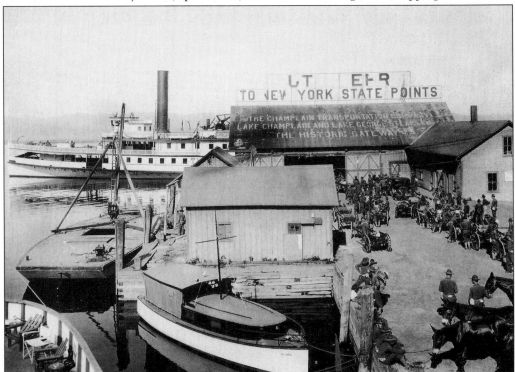

The *Ticonderoga* carried more than tourists. When these cavalry troops prepared to board the steamer for transport to Plattsburgh Training Camp in 1938, the United States was only three years from becoming involved in World War II.

Lake Champlain ferries also transported military equipment during the Cold War. In the 1950s, several trucks carrying sections of an Air Force plane boarded the *Valcour*.

Every few years, snowmelt and spring rains raise the lake above dock level, delaying the opening of the Burlington/Port Kent ferry.

Two
Downstreet

This is a view from the belfry of the Unitarian Church, looking south, *c.* 1860. The main business district was still along Battery Street. Church Street was a mix of shops and private homes, including that of George Perkins Marsh in the foreground on the east corner of Church Street. The First Congregational Church on South Winooski Avenue, built in 1842, is visible at far left.

City Hall Park, shown here about 1865, was originally called "Court House Square." Visible to the north, from left to right, are: the First Baptist Church, built in 1864; St. Paul's Episcopal Church, built in 1832; and the Cathedral of the Immaculate Conception, built during 1863–67. "Bank Block" was on the north side of the park. On the east were Lyman King's Tavern and the county courthouse.

By the 1890s, City Hall Park had become square-shaped and had gained sidewalks. On the east side are the Ethan Allen firehouse, the court house, and City Hall, which was built in 1853 and torn down in 1925 to make way for the present building.

Shown in a 1906 postcard, the City Hall Park fountain was donated by John P. Howard and erected in September 1881. A generation later, Mayor James E. Burke kept brook trout in the fountain as summer "pets."

City employees install electric lamps in City Hall Park on June 4, 1938, while onlookers enjoy the shade of the elms. The project was funded by the Works Progress Administration.

Built in 1870 on the site of the old Howard House, which had burned in 1867, the Van Ness House occupied the southwest corner of Main and St. Paul Streets until it, too, burned in 1951. It was enlarged in 1882 and 1892 and could accommodate four hundred guests. The site is now a branch of the Howard Bank.

The Hotel Vermont, one of the tallest buildings in the state, was built on the former location of the American House (an annex of the Van Ness), which closed in 1893 after sixty years. The hotel was later sold to the University of Vermont (UVM) and converted to apartments.

Hotel Burlington was rebuilt in 1887 by George M. Delaney on the west side of St. Paul Street facing City Hall Park, where the Huntington Apartments stand today. It accommodated one hundred and fifty guests. Like so many other structures on this block, it, too, burned.

The New Sherwood Hotel, on the corner of Church and Cherry Streets, appears here in a 1920s postcard. It burned on February 13, 1937. The site was later occupied by Sears Roebuck and more recently by the J.C. Penney department store.

This is a northerly view up Church Street at College Street about 1910. Electric trolley cars went into service in 1893, run by the Burlington Traction Company. The trolleys were replaced by motorized bus service in 1929, which offered somewhat more comfort and flexibility. A mock funeral was held on August 4, 1929, and a trolley was ceremoniously burned in front of Hotel Vermont.

By the 1950s, the dominance of the automobile was long-standing. Church Street, shown here at Main Street looking north, resembled most American towns. The Hitching Post restaurant, at right, was a popular hangout for high school students after classes.

An easterly view up College Street about 1920 shows the distant spire of College Street Congregational Church. In the foreground at left is the Howard Bank, built in 1902. The Burlington Free Press Building, dating from the 1880s, is in the middle of the block at right.

Founded with a donation from Mrs. Mary L. Fletcher and her daughter, Miss Mary M. Fletcher, the Fletcher Free Library opened July 6, 1875. It soon outgrew its original quarters in the old courthouse and in 1904 moved into a new brick building on College Street at South Winooski, donated principally by Andrew Carnegie.

Prominent in this view up Main Street from the roof of the Hotel Vermont about 1920 are, clockwise: old City Hall (left), Fletcher Free Library, College Street Congregational Church, Edmunds High School, the Strong Theater, and the U.S. Customs House and Post Office.

The United States Custom House and Post Office on Main Street was built of Vermont marble and granite in 1906. This 1920s view also shows the county court house at right, built in 1872 of local purple sandstone and destroyed by fire in 1982. When the federal agencies moved to Elmwood Avenue and Pearl Street in 1960, the court moved into the imposing marble building to its north.

The Strong Block opened October 24, 1904, on the southwest corner of Main and South Winooski Streets. It housed the Strong Theater, which seated fifteen hundred people, law offices, and a paint store and hardware store on the ground floor. The block was destroyed by fire in 1970, and the site stood empty for several years. Since 1988, it has been the location of Court House Plaza.

Burlington's first "town-city hall," built in 1854, was razed in 1925 to make room for construction of the present City Hall. The police, pauper, and liquor departments occupied the basement. The new City Hall also displaced the county courthouse, at left, which had been built jointly in 1830 by the county and the town.

The Masonic Temple, on the west corner of Church and Pearl Streets, was built in 1898, partly to attract substantial citizens to settle in Burlington. A high proportion of prominent men in the city were Masons, as well as members of other fraternal organizations. The building was sold in 1983 to the law firm of Paul, Frank, and Collins.

Built at the same time as the City Hall in 1925, Memorial Auditorium was dedicated to those residents who fought in World War I. The structure could seat three thousand people and is still the city's largest auditorium. The Burlington Water Department meter room was located in the basement.

Following a January fire, the old YMCA Building on the corner of Church and College Streets was built in 1887–88 jointly with Samuel Huntington, whose bookstore was on the ground level. Fire again destroyed all but the first floor in 1928, and the "Y" moved to South Union Street. MacAuliffe Paper Company and bookstore rebuilt the structure, now occupied by Michael Kehoe Ltd. and the Merchants Bank.

Shown here in 1940, Valade's Terminal Restaurant, across from the City Hall Park, also attracted many customers who were not bus travelers. The corner of Main and St. Paul Streets has been home to a succession of restaurants, most recently the Bagel Bakery, which burned in 1996.

Ammi B. Young, who designed the Vermont statehouse in Montpelier, was hired by Timothy Follett to build this Greek Revival mansion overlooking the waterfront in 1847. After Follett's fortunes failed, the house had several owners, including the Adams Mission, 1895–1905; a rooming house for young women, 1905–1917; the Knights of Columbus, 1927–1941; and the Veterans of Foreign Wars, 1948–1979.

After narrowly avoiding destruction by arson on May 30, 1979, the Follett mansion remains a reminder of Burlington's nineteenth-century glory days as a major center of commerce.

Three
Views Around Town

Prominent residents chose the "Hill Section" for their stately homes, as this *c.* 1890 photograph of South Willard Street shows. C.P. Smith, president of Burlington Savings Bank, built the home on the right.

Horses were still the preferred mode of transportation around 1915, although automobiles were becoming more common, as seen in this view of Main Street, up from Willard Street. Note the hitching posts on the left.

The George Linsley house was located one in from the corner of Pearl on South Williams Streets next to the home of Elihu Taft. The ladies on the porch are Linsley's wife, Faustina, and daughter, Mary. The third woman is unidentified. Both houses were later torn down to make way for Taft School.

United States Senator George F. Edmunds erected his home on the southwest corner of Main and South Willard Streets. It was occupied by the principal of Edmunds High School in 1905.

One of the oldest brick houses in the city is located at 288 Main Street. Built by Mark Rice about 1806, its "bomb-proof cellar" was used as a safe deposit for city records during the War of 1812. This photograph was taken about 1956.

Long-time Burlington residents will recognize this structure as "the Bishop's House." Demolished during the 1980s to make way for DeGoesbriand parking lot, this impressive residence was built by D.C. Linsley.

Although A.E. Richardson was best known for his association with Wells, Richardson and Co, he was also a partner of W.B. McKillip, a local lawyer involved in real estate. Richardson purchased the D.C. Linsley house on South Williams Street and may have added the turret.

Burlington lawyer Henry Ballard erected this house at 285 South Willard in 1889 and lived here until 1902, the approximate date of the photograph. Frank D. Abernethy of Abernethy's Department Store purchased the dwelling in June 1916.

The Edward Wells house on South Willard Street. Wells was a wholesale druggist in the family firm of Wells, Richardson and Co. The company's most popular tonic, Paine's Celery Compound, was touted as "Nature's True Remedy."

Expansive lawns, large estates, and orchards graced South Prospect Street during the nineteenth century. Although sidewalks had been installed for pedestrian travel, the roadway was still unpaved.

During 1859, Col. LeGrand B. Cannon built this French chateau on 40 acres of land between South Willard and South Prospect Streets. The house burned long ago; the only remaining structure from the former estate is a stone coachman's cottage. By combining the Lake Champlain Steamboat line with the Delaware & Hudson Railroad, Cannon provided passenger and freight service to New York City.

Redstone, the home of A.A. Buell, later gave its name to the University of Vermont's Redstone Campus and is now owned by the University. The stone was quarried at the Willard Quarry off Shelburne Road. During 1900, when the photo was taken, Redstone was known for its well-landscaped grounds.

BURLINGTON COUNTRY CLUB. BURLINGTON. VT.

Organized in 1925, the Burlington Country Club is located on South Prospect Street south of Redstone Campus. A favorite course for golfers during the summer, the club's hilly terrain has always been popular with sledders and tobogganers.

Although trolley cars provided public transportation, horses were still a very important mode of travel around 1900. Note the hitching posts in front on several houses on the left side of the street.

This house was the residence of Oscar Heininger on College Street. Built by the Kieslich Construction Company, the home is a fine example of Craftsman architecture. Today, it used for offices.

The Moore-Woodbury house at 416 Pearl was built about 1815 by George Moore, a Pearl Street merchant and one of the originators of the Burlington Woolen Co. at Winooski Falls. The house was purchased by Urban A. Woodbury in 1886. Shown in 1889, when Woodbury was lieutenant governor, the house was the scene for many social events. Presidents William McKinley, Theodore Roosevelt, and William Howard Taft were guests of the Woodburys.

Green Mountain Cemetery, situated on a hill overlooking Winooski, is one of the oldest cemeteries in the city and is the resting place of Gen. Ethan Allen. Dedicated on July 4, 1873, a 42-foot-high monument marks his grave.

Landscaped as a park in 1853, Battery Park was originally the parade ground of the 15th Infantry Regiment commanded by Captain Zebulon Montgomery Pike during the War of 1812. The Army sold the land in 1831, and in 1840, Heman Allen, N.B. Haswell, Frederick Smith, and W.H. Wilkins deeded the land to the town.

Battery Park has always been a favorite place to enjoy the view of the Adirondacks. Photographed in 1923 by Erna Heininger, Miss Kate Snow is seated near one of four naval cannons sent by Annapolis in May of 1895. Three of the cannons were sold for scrap in 1941.

Ethan Allen Tower was dedicated on August 16, 1905, shortly before the photograph was taken. Erected on a bluff near the entrance of Ethan Allen's original farm, the site was formerly known as "Indian Rock." William Van Patten purchased the land in 1902. Roads in the park were laid out by Van Patten and his Morgan horse, Mattie, who sought the easiest trails to ascend the bluff.

The city purchased North Beach, a large wooded area, and also an open field from the Arthur farm on July 17, 1918. The bathhouse was built at a cost of $2,000 in 1919. The campground was in operation at the time of this 1920s postcard.

The Central Vermont Railroad opened Queen City Park for use by its employees for picnics. The Spiritualist Corporation purchased the property in 1880, providing a hotel, pavilion, cottages, and recreational facilities for its guests.

The Hotel at Queen City Park, Burlington, Vt.

Burlington photographer L.L. McAllister served as president of the local Spiritualists, whose hotel, shown in this 1900 postcard, was the center for the organization's summer activities. The hotel burned in 1939 and was never rebuilt.

Some parts of Burlington appear much as they did fifty years ago. The rotary at the intersection of South Union Street, South Willard Street, and Shelburne Street has undergone few changes since this 1942 photograph was taken. A real estate office has replaced the gas station, however.

Other areas of Burlington have changed immensely. In 1930, farmland surrounded the intersection of upper Main Street and what is now East Avenue.

The Route 7 Winooski-Burlington Highway Bridge was built to replace the span destroyed by the 1927 flood. It was the largest deck-plate girder in Vermont at the time of its construction in 1928.

It is easy to see why early settlers were attracted to the Winooski Valley and its rich land on the valley floor. Several farms were operating in the valley in 1905.

Four

Getting Around

The Winooski & Burlington Horse Railroad Co. operated between 6 and 7 miles of street railroad. With the Van Ness House as the hub, lines ran to Winooski, Lake View Cemetery, and the Burlington Cotton Mills.

The Burlington Bus Company ran a bus between Burlington and Cambridge Junction from the early 1920s to 1938, when the Vermont Transit bought them out. Vermont Transit extended the route to Portland, Maine.

Electric trolley cars gave way to buses during the 1920s in a cost-cutting move by Burlington Rapid Transit. Although many felt the trolley was clean and efficient, operating costs were high because the cars required a great deal of horsepower.

In 1940, the Central Terminal adjacent to Valade's at Main and St. Paul Streets afforded travelers one-stop shopping for bus, train, and airplane tickets.

The interior of the Central Terminal during the 1940s included a coffee shop that served travelers and local residents.

Built on the waterfront during 1861 by Daniel Linsley, the Central Vermont Railroad Terminal enabled shipments of freight and passengers to transfer easily to and from lake transportation. George Linsley's coal yard supplied fuel to stoke the steam-powered locomotives. Shepard & Morse Lumber Co. owned 4,000 feet of dock frontage at which thirty to thirty-five vessels could unload at one time.

The Central Vermont locomotive No. 231 is on the barge canal bridge in this 1890 picture. Originally the *Burlington* of the Burlington & Lamoille Railroad from 1877 to 1889, this engine was renamed the Rutland Railroad No. 73 in 1896.

46

Increased passenger traffic prompted Burlington's business community to negotiate with the railroads for a larger train station. A plan was approved in 1914, and the new Union Station opened in January of 1915. By 1926, freight and passenger trains passing through Burlington numbered 20,075.

Union Station was designed by Feilhelmer & Long of New York City. During the 1920s, a local newspaper reported that on a single day, eighteen hundred passengers passed through the building in 24 minutes.

The *Francis Saltus* was built in 1844. The vessel was a victim of rate wars and then piracy, when previous owners stole the paddleboat to keep it from operating on the lake. The *Francis Saltus* was scuttled at Shelburne Shipyard because of an ownership dispute in 1856.

The *Reindeer* is moored at Burlington harbor. Built in 1882, it was the only steamboat operating on Lake Champlain that was not the property of Champlain Transportation Company.

The *Vermont III* was built in 1903 at the Shelburne Shipyard. She was 262 feet long and was the tallest steamboat on Lake Champlain. The bridge in Addison was built to accommodate the vessel's height. Although the ship was a favorite of passengers, it was losing money by 1930. The boat was later gutted and redesigned as an Atlantic Coast diesel freighter.

The steamers *Vermont* and *Ticonderoga* meet at Burlington harbor, *c.* 1910.

The first steel-hulled steamer on Lake Champlain, the *Chateaugay* was built in 1888. Converted to an automobile ferry in 1925, the ship was later redesigned and is now running as the *Mount Washington III* on Lake Winnepesaukee in New Hampshire.

Built in 1906, the *Ticonderoga* ferried passengers between Vermont and New York. It saw servic as an excursion boat after World War II.

At the urging of Ralph Nading Hill, Electra Havemeyer Webb purchased the *Ticonderoga* for the Shelburne Museum. A railbed was constructed, and the steamer moved over land during the winter months of 1954. The *Ticonderoga* was restored and is now on display at the Shelburne Museum.

Champlain Transportation Co. ceased operating steamboats in 1938, and they began using ferries solely designed for transporting motor vehicles.

This aerial view shows the *City of Burlington* entering Burlington harbor. Built in 1936, the diesel-screw-powered boat ran from Burlington to Port Kent and Port Douglas.

The *Adirondack* is shown landing at Port Kent, New York, *c.* 1956. Originally named the *Governor Emerson C. Harrington*, the ferry was built in 1913 in Jacksonville, Florida, and is still in operation today.

Operational since September 22, 1921, Burlington Airport is located on the former site of the University of Vermont tree farm. The hangar was completed June 1, 1929, and could house six planes ready for flight or ten planes prepared for storage. Professor Arthur D. Butterfield, Alderman John J. Burnes, and Alfred H. Heininger were the first airport commissioners.

Colonial Airlines was one of the first carriers to offer regular service from the airport. Harold Pugh served as airport manager from 1932 to 1943. Pugh's wife Grace was also a pilot, and the pair operated the Fli-Rite School of Aviation, which was part of the Civilian Pilot Training Program. Fli-Rite trained combat pilots during World War II.

As air travel gained in popularity, the airport updated its facilities in 1939 and added a new south wing to the administration building in 1945. Air traffic control came to the airport in April of 1942. A "temporary" tower was built during the fall of that year and remained in service until 1950, when it was torn down.

Planning for airport improvements began in 1946. A new administration building was completed at a cost of $225,000 in 1949 and dedicated on January 1, 1950. This aerial photo shows construction in process on the 7,000-foot extension of the diagonal runway in 1951.

Five
Earning a Living

Designed by Daniel Linsley, the earthen reservoir, on the hilltop south of UVM, was under construction in the autumn of 1867. It held 2.25 million gallons. The pumping station is located on Main Street across from Morrill Hall.

In 1894, the Water Department extended the raw water intake from near the breakwater out to Appletree Reef. The iron intake pipe was 2 feet in diameter and is still in use.

Experienced divers connected the pipes beneath the surface of the lake. The diver, Harry Longley, is about to resume underwater work on the 1894 pipeline. The spotter, J.G. Falcon, remained on the barge, keeping track of the air hose, pump, and lifeline.

This is a photograph of a city-owned portable steam-driven water pump, *c.* 1890. This pump was considered state-of-the-art because of its perceived ease of transport and operation.

The Water Department's meter room was in the basement of the new Memorial Auditorium in 1928. The meters were later moved to the new water plant. At right is Leo Dion.

A portion of the Queen City Cotton Company's non-union work force of six hundred poses before the mill on Lake Street about 1914. Rising competition from Southern mills and a 1934 workers' strike spelled the end for the Burlington plant, forcing the company to dissolve in

A gleaming carriage showroom on Front Street in 1910 already houses the automobile, at rear, that will make carriages obsolete.

1940. In 1943, Bell Aircraft Corporation leased the building for its ordnance division and by 1944 employed 2,700 workers. General Electric owned the facility from 1947 until the mid-1980s. Weapons, such as fighter planes, are still manufactured in the plant.

The carriage shop proprietor is flanked by two employees. The men are wearing jodhpurs and leggings.

This is a photograph of workers, mainly French-Canadian, inside the Queen City Cotton mill, c. 1900. Built in 1894, this model factory at peak production used 1,300 Northop automatic looms, a new style of looms never before used, to weave sateen and cotton twill fabrics. Its payroll of six hundred workers made it Burlington's largest taxpayer.

The daughters of a prominent sail-maker, the Wakefield sisters are wearing cotton and linen summer dresses in a style popular for young ladies around 1900. Sarah (left) and Mary (right) are seated; standing, from left to right, are Lavinia, Emma Wakefield McIntire, and Henryetta Wakefield Linsley. Their father risked his life when he rowed out to rescue the passengers of the *General Butler*, which had wrecked on the breakwater during a storm.

This is a postcard showing the interior of the Park Cafe & Sea Grill about 1930. The cafe was located on Main Street across from City Hall Park.

The wait staff, kitchen staff, and management pose in front of the Black Cat Cafe on Bank Street, c. 1930s. The cafe burned, along with the State Theater and the rest of the block during a fire in the 1970s.

This is a photograph of people cutting ice in 1940 at the Burlington water treatment plant. Before the age of refrigeration, blocks of lake ice were pulled on horse-drawn sleds to storage buildings near the waterfront. To right of the stack, on the hill, is a car dealership, later Acme

A city street-cleaning crew poses for photographer L.L. McAllister in 1930. The location is believed to be on North Union Street.

Paint & Glass, now the Burlington police headquarters. The white building on the top left is Colodny's Market.

After the disastrous 1927 flood, the Civilian Conservation Corps provided valuable labor for building flood control dams in the Winooski Valley during the 1930s. This work crew of young men was camped at Queen City Park.

This is the main switchboard at Bell Telephone Company's College Street building, 1935. Working as an operator was considered suitable, even ideal, employment for women.

Burlington Daily News paper-carriers pose on College Street in the 1940s. The *Daily News* first appeared by 1894, founded by Col. H. Nelson Jackson. The paper was sold in 1940 to William Loeb, who had recently bought the *St. Albans Messenger*. Loeb's local witch-hunting and crusades alienated advertisers, and the paper died in 1961.

The owner and employees of Hathorne Roofers pose in front of their van and building on South Winooski, about where the *Free Press* loading dock is located today. Hathorne was the preferred roofer for Burlington contractors.

Peter DiSpirito (on left), maintenance foreman, and Peter Perino study plans during construction of the parking lot at General Electric on Lake Street, 1950. The workman at right is unidentified.

One of the first "remote" radio broadcasts in Burlington was done by Val Carter of WDOT. The three-hour program included music and information about used cars at Colonial Motors Chrysler-Plymouth at Pine and Main Streets (later Lake View Buick). Used car sales manager Bill Gilbertson reported record-breaking one-day sales, and the trend was set.

At Kresge's Department Store's soda fountain in the 1950s, a full lunch cost 55¢ to 60¢. Kresge's was on Church Street between Bank and Cherry Streets, now the entrance to the Burlington Square Mall.

Six

Daily Life

Although cars were less numerous than today, driving in 1920 had its hazards. The driver of this automobile negotiated a turn onto College Street with too much speed.

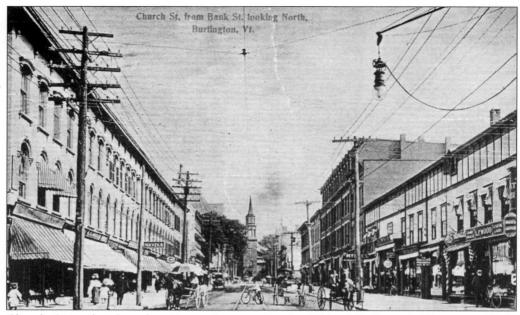

Church Street has long been a retail center for the City of Burlington. The spire of the Unitarian Church is visible in the background of this *c*. 1900 postcard.

During the nineteenth century, all of the city's fire companies were manned by volunteers. This 1890s photograph shows an unidentified company wearing full dress uniform. It may have been taken at the intersection of Pearl and Church Streets.

Lake Champlain from "Red Rocks", Burlington, Vt.

Strolls along the lakeside have always been a favorite past-time of residents and visitors alike. People dressed more formally for their outings during the 1890s, as these fashionable ladies demonstrate in this postcard.

The rock formations around Rock Point are best seen from the lake. Today, few boaters would consider suits, ties, and bowler hats necessary attire. However, during the latter part of the nineteenth century, these men were properly dressed for the activity.

The Ethan Allen homestead was still a working farm in 1910. Owned by a Tory prior to the Revolutionary War, the land was confiscated by the "Republic of Vermont" and sold to General Ethan Allen. Restored to its original state during the 1980s, the house is now part of a living history museum on the site.

Erna Heininger (standing on right) and unidentified companions visited the gardens of Mrs. Pease (seated) during the 1920s. Only since World War II has the custom of making afternoon visits gone out of fashion.

The extension of the breakwater brought pedestrians further into the lake. During the 1920s, it was considered a good spot for fishing and relaxing.

Miss Helen Ludwig enjoys North Beach during the mid-1920s in this picture. The bathhouse rented swimming suits and lockers. North Beach has long been considered the best sandy beach in Chittenden County.

Street and sidewalk upgrades inconvenience this pedestrian on South Winooski Avenue in 1931. Foot travel was still a popular means of transportation.

Long lines of shoppers were common when nylon hosiery went on sale during World War II. Prospective customers at this North Street store seem deceptively calm.

The 1940s heralded an era of shorter skirts and sleeker cars. The brick building on the right housed the jail.

The Miss Burlington Diner, located on the east side of Winooski Avenue just north of College Street, was frequented by many of the downtown business people. These diners were photographed on February 10, 1941.

A corner of the smoking room shows the opulence of the Ethan Allen Club. Originally founded in 1848 as the Ethan Allen Fire Engine Company No. 4, the name was changed to the Ethan Allen Club on November 11, 1896. The club's focus changed from protecting property against fires to promoting an intellectually stimulating social organization. The "Ethans" were known as the "silk stocking crowd" because most of the members were bankers, merchants, and businessmen.

In 1905, the Ethan Allen Club purchased the J.H. Peck property on College Street. President William Howard Taft attended a club luncheon in July 1906 and was made an honorary member in 1909. This house burned on December 5, 1971. The club reopened in new, larger quarters on November 2, 1972.

Radio programs like this one featuring Burlington Mayor John J. Burns (right) being interviewed by WJOY's Bob Beaupre, city editor, kept the community informed. Mayor from 1939 to 1948, Burns was a pioneer in aviation and during a term as alderman, was instrumental in the building of the municipal airport.

Opened by Louis and Victoria Bove during the 1940s, Italian meals at Bove's restaurant at 68 Pearl Street attracted customers from all over the region. Victoria developed the sauce recipe that has made Bove's famous. This 1930 photo shows Victoria with her daughter Jane.

PIZZA
(SERVES 2)

WITH PEPPERONI	.95
WITH CHEESE	.85
WITH ANCHOVIES (FISH)	.95
WITH MEAT BALLS	1.00
WITH ONIONS	.95

Sandwich Suggestions

Special Open Steak Sandwich on Toast with Salad	**.75**
Meat Ball Set-up THREE (3) MEAT BALLS, SAUCE, ITALIAN CHEESE, BREAD AND BUTTER	**.40**
STEAK SANDWICH	.45
ITALIAN CHEESE	.35
ITALIAN SALAMI	.35
PEPPERONI AND EGG	.35
ITALIAN MEAT BALL	.30
CHEESEBURGER	.35
GRILLED CHEESE	.20
HAMBURG	.30
TUNA FISH	.35
BACON, LETTUCE AND TOMATO	.35
BACON AND EGG	.35
BACON	.25
LETTUCE AND TOMATO	.20
WESTERN	.35
EASTERN	.30
BOSTON	.30
FRIED HAM	.35
EGG, HAM AND CHEESE	.50

Drinks

COCA COLA (BOTTLE)		.15
ORANGE JUICE (LARGE)		.20
COFFEE		.10
MILK (WHITE OR CHOCOLATE)		.10
GINGER ALE (PER GLASS)		.10
7-UP (BOTTLE)		.15
TOMATO JUICE (LARGE)		.20
TEA OR ICED TEA	.10	.15

Bove's menu in 1950 introduced pizza to Burlington. The prices are for a whole pizza.

Photographed in 1951, Miss Alice Schoffstall assisted patrons of the Fletcher Free Library for many years.

Prior to Saturday morning cartoons on television, special children's matinees were sponsored by local radio stations. These 1940s youngsters are enjoying a show hosted by Val Carter at the Strong Theater.

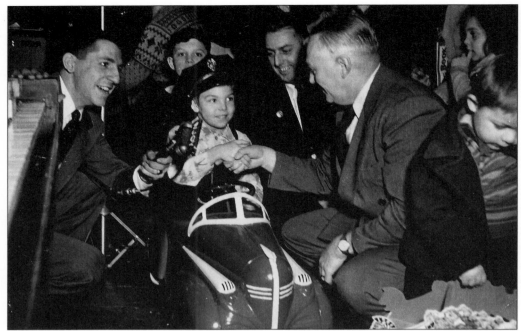

Mayor J. Edward Moran (right) and popular WJOY host Val Carter attend a party for underprivileged children broadcast from the State Theater on Christmas Eve in 1949. Carter's radio show, "Magic Eye," helped children in forty Vermont and New York cities and towns get ready for school each morning.

Val Carter and Roger LaRoche, manager and chief engineer of WDOT, are in contact with a plane from the 37th Interceptor Fighter Squadron. Thousands of Burlington residents listened to the historic "Operation Intercept" broadcast aired live during the 1950s.

78

Seven
Learning

This is the Class of 1905 at Burlington Grammar School. Among those pictured are Charles Smith (back row, fifth from left), Robert Adsit (fourth row, second from right), Edward Crane (fourth row, third from right), and George Fremeau (fifth row, third from left). The school had six teachers and two hundred students.

Shown about 1900, the eight-room Converse School was located on the southwest corner of Pine and Cherry Streets, with a large playground fronting on Champlain Street. Built in 1893, the school had ten teachers and three hundred and fifty pupils.

Ira Allen School was built in 1894 on the north side of Colchester Avenue, opposite Mary Fletcher Hospital. Four teachers taught one hundred and twenty students.

Pomeroy School, on North and Booth Streets, was built in 1874 and doubled in size in 1898. In the 1920s, the schoolyard was the the site of the Redpath Chautauqua, a traveling tent show which performed for one week each summer. Today the corner is a neighborhood park.

The Hebrew Free School at 255 North Winooski Avenue was dedicated on January 15, 1905. Over one hundred boys attended similar schools in the Hyde Street synagogue and in private homes to prepare for bar mitzvah.

The Roman Catholic Nazareth School, on Allen Street opposite St. Joseph Church, was founded in 1869 and continued to 1929.

At the 1925 Nazareth School graduation, shown on the Elmwood Avenue rectory steps, the rector, Father Norbert Proulx, is at center with Father E. Alloit, S.S.E., of St Michael's, at right. The tall girl just above "per aspera" is Kathleen Langlois, now Sister Mary Leocardia, R.S.M. of St. Mary's.

Cathedral School, on the southwest corner of St. Paul and Cherry Streets, was dedicated September 1, 1901 and served more than five hundred pupils. It was closed in 1959 and razed in the 1960s during urban renewal.

Shown here about 1890, Burlington Union High School was built in 1871 on the site of an earlier 1816 academy on the northwest corner of College and South Willard Streets. The grammar school shared the building until Edmunds High School was built in 1900.

Built on land at Main and South Union Streets donated by George F. Edmunds in 1898, Edmunds High School opened on May 2, 1900. It accommodated six hundred students. Shown in 1957, the student safety patrol members (pictured wearing sashes) were, from left to right, Tony Wasilkowski, Gordon Perlmutter, Saul Likowski, David Cunningham, John Bergeron, and Louis DiSpirito. Edmunds High became a junior high or "middle school" when the new high school opened in 1964.

Originally the Providence Orphan Asylum and Hospital, St. Joseph's Orphan Asylum began housing children in 1884. These orphans and the elderly were cared for by the Sisters of Providence (Montreal) until 1982. The structure has been added to and renovated several times, and today it is the Catholic diocese's administration building.

Mount St. Mary's gymnasium, *c.* 1935, was used extensively by Trinity College students.

Mann Hall at Trinity College, built in 1939–40, was the dormitory, library, classroom, and dining room for these student skiers, shown about 1945. It was named after Mother Mary Emmanuel (Frances Mann), dean of the college and later mother superior, 1941–47 and 1953–57.

Two of Trinity College's founders were: Mother Mary Alphonsus (Ellen Cassidy), on the left; and Mother Mary Magdalen (Alice Delehanty), on the right, who was the first president of the college.

These students watch the 1958 construction of Trinity's McAuley Hall, named after Mother Catherine McAuley, founder of the Sisters of Mercy in Dublin in 1831.

The University of Vermont Class of 1908 sported fake Victorian-era whiskers at their 25th reunion in 1933. Alfred Heininger is in the front row, second from right.

"Old Stone Row" is shown above about 1905. Billings Library, on the left, designed by Henry Hobson Richardson and built during 1883–85, was the UVM library until 1961. Williams Science Hall, constructed to be completely fireproof in 1896, was renovated in 1972 as the university art department. The Old Mill, on the right, began as three separate structures in 1825; they were united in 1846 to form one long building. A fourth story and the octagonal steeple were added in 1882–83.

Named to commemorate UVM's benefactor and designed by McKim, Mead & White, the university's official architects, Ira Allen Chapel was completed in 1926. The bell tower is 170 feet high, a landmark for any traveler to Burlington.

Eight
Religion

A 1953 mass to mark the Burlington diocese's 100th year was celebrated at the Roman Catholic Cathedral of the Immaculate Conception. The celebrant was the apostolic delegate to the United States, Archbishop Amleto G. Cicognani.

Located at the northwest corner of Cherry and St. Paul Streets, the Cathedral of the Immaculate Conception was dedicated December 8, 1867, after four years of construction. It was destroyed by fire March 13–14, 1972, a great loss to the community.

Still the largest church in Vermont, the imposing St. Joseph Church formally opened on Easter Sunday, 1887. It was consecrated on August 22, 1901, when the marble altar was dedicated. The largely French-Canadian Catholic congregation was organized in 1850.

This is a view of St. Joseph Church's interior as it appeared about 1890.

Bishop Edward F. Ryan celebrated mass on August 10, 1955, to mark his fiftieth jubilee. Exiting the cathedral, from left to right, are: Msgr. Crosby, Msgr. L'Ecuyer, Bishop Ryan, unidentified trainbearer, Edward Foster (holding cross), O. Dufault and Edward Buckly (acolytes), Msgr. Mishelke (with glasses), Msgr. Kennedy, and Archbishop Richard Cushing.

Joseph Lechnyr, shown about 1950, conducted the Catholic cathedral choir for many years. He also directed bands, orchestras, and choruses in the parish, as well as the UVM R.O.T.C. band. Lechnyr began his career as a U.S. Army bandmaster in World War I.

St. Paul's Episcopal Cathedral occupied much of the block between St. Paul and Pine Streets, north of Bank Street, for one hundred and forty years, until it was destroyed by fire February 15, 1971. This view was taken about 1905.

Burlington's First Congregational Church on South Winooski Avenue was organized in 1805. After its building burned in 1839, the congregation replaced it in 1842 with the present Greek Revival-style structure, shown here in 1905.

LEFT: The Unitarian Church, shown about 1890, was built in 1816 from plans by Charles Bulfinch on 2.25 acres donated by Horace Loomis and E.T. Englesby for the purpose of building the church. The clock was installed in the church tower in 1872.

RIGHT: The church choir, *c.* 1875, included Mrs. Nash, Edward Lyman, Col. Hindes, and Miss Barlow.

Organized in 1860, a third Congregational Society erected the stone Gothic-style College Street Congregational Church in 1865–66, which still stands at the southwest corner of South Union Street.

Nine
Health Care

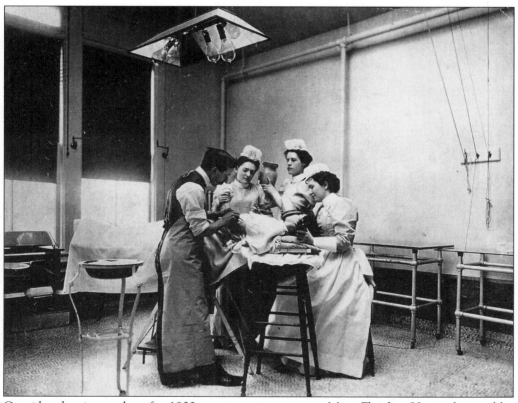

Considered quite modern for 1900, an operating room at Mary Fletcher Hospital resembles little the surgical suites of the 1990s. The nurse seated at right is Minnie Hollister, who later became the wife of Dr. R.G. Perry. Miss Hollister graduated from Mary Fletcher Hospital School of Nursing in 1900.

Selected as the best site for the hospital, the Catlin Farm was purchased for $25,000. The main building (left) and men's ward (center) cost $50,000 to build in 1879 and had a total of twenty-nine beds. The nurses' residence was constructed in 1896 for $12,000, and it burned in 1948.

Mary Martha Fletcher fulfilled her family's dream of building a hospital. Born in 1830, Miss Fletcher was the sole heir to her parents' fortune. Although she had tuberculosis, she decided to spend her fortune on the care of others. When she died in 1885, Miss Fletcher was a patient at the hospital that bore her name.

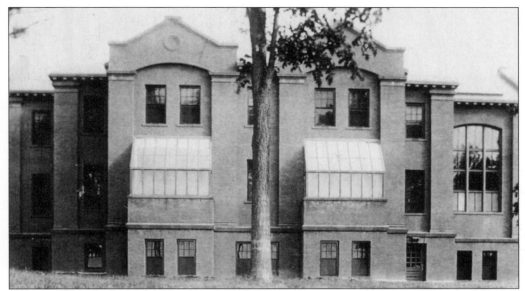

Mary Fletcher Hospital added the surgical building and the Private Pavilion (now part of Brown Pavilion) between 1907 and 1908, for a total cost of $180,000.

Kieslich Construction Co. was in charge of the construction of Bishop de Goesbriand Memorial Hospital. Named after the Rt. Rev. Louis de Goesbriand, the first Roman Catholic Bishop of Burlington, the 188-bed hospital opened in September 1925. It is now the University Health Center division of Fletcher Allen Health Care.

LEFT: Edmund Towle Brown, M.D., was the attending clinical surgeon of eye, ear, nose, and throat at the three area hospitals, as well as a professor of medicine at the University of Vermont. Dr. Brown also served as the physician for the residents of the Home for Destitute Children and Home for Friendless Women during the 1920s.

RIGHT: Bird Joseph Arthur Bombard, M.D., began practicing medicine in Burlington during 1906. A well-known surgeon, Dr. Bombard served as alderman in 1907–1908 and was later appointed chairman of the city Board of Health, which he held from 1918 to 1925.

Originally called the Medical Center Building, the Patrick and Smith Wings were built in 1952 for $2,700,000. The new addition was designed by the architectural firm of McKim, Mead and White, the designers of Burlington City Hall, Fleming Museum, Ira Allen Chapel, Southwick, and Waterman Buildings.

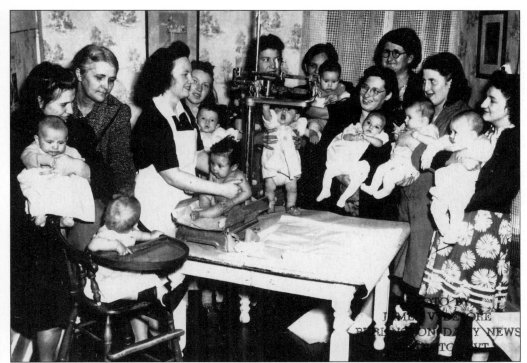

Burlington health officials have held Well-Baby Clinics since the early 1900s. This 1950 clinic was held at the Burlington Community Center at 16 Cherry Street. The name of the center was changed to Sara Holbrook Community Center in 1958 to honor its founder. It moved to its present location on North Street during 1966.

The Visiting Nurse Association (VNA) has long assisted ill, recovering, disabled, and elderly patients in their homes. This 1949 nurse has just left the home of a patient.

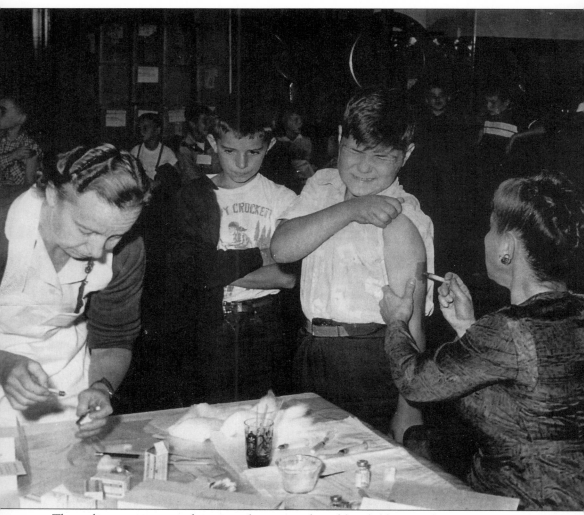

The polio vaccine was administered to more than fifty children at this VNA immunization clinic on March 2, 1958. Some clinics vaccinated as many as a hundred children against the dreaded disease, which maimed and killed thousands nationally during each epidemic. Miss Emily Dinegan was the director of the VNA at the time of this photograph.

Ten
Characters

Lawrence Barnes arrived in the village of Burlington in 1855 and started a lumber yard in 1856. By the 1870s, the company was doing $4,000,000 in annual business. Barnes bought Grasse Mount in 1866 and lived there till his death in 1883. He became the first president of the Howard Bank in 1870.

Frederick M. Van Sicklin was a South Burlington boy who entered the wholesale grocery business in 1856 and went on to become the senior partner in the firm of Van Sicklin & Seymore, located in the Old Stone Store at the intersection of Battery and King Streets. From 1886 until his death, he was also president of the Howard National Bank.

Cyrus M. Spaulding was one of Van Sicklin's partners in the Old Stone Store. His other business activities included banking, railroads, and the Champlain Transportation Company.

J.D. Hatch retired from his successful general store in Windsor and moved to Burlington in 1861. While in the city, he was an alderman from 1870 until 1876, when he was elected mayor. He held this position for seven years, longer than any of his predecessors. Hatch had a very large circle of friends among the powerful politicians of his day, and when the state legislature was in session, he lobbied on behalf of the Central Vermont Railroad.

Miss Francis S. Forbes married J.D. Hatch in Windsor on April 5, 1832. Prior to her death in 1883, she was considered one of the most genial hostesses in Burlington.

George L. Linsley had a varied career as a railroad contractor in his youth and as a coal merchant in his middle age (see top photo, page 46). One of his most unusual projects involved the expansion of the Central Vermont's lakeshore rail yards. Fifteen acres of additional waterfront property were created using the fill washed down from the Battery Park bluff. High-pressure water guns broke up the soil, which was then carried to the lakeshore by a network of flumes.

This is Faustina Wright Linsley, George's wife. Didn't she have a lovely name? Mrs. Linsley was one of the founders of the Converse Home.

Daniel C. Linsley, George's older brother, was a nationally known railroad contractor and civil engineer. Linsley designed New York's Third Avenue elevated railway. His Vermont projects included the survey of the first Mount Mansfield toll road, Burlington's first reservoir, and the 340-foot railroad tunnel under North Avenue, the construction of which he supervised in 1861. At one time, eleven trains used the route daily, but rail traffic declined and the last passenger train passed through the tunnel June 16, 1938.

Martha "Pattie" Linsley, the daughter of Mr. and Mrs. J.D. Hatch, was Daniel's wife. Daniel's sister Eliza, after meeting Pattie for the first time, wrote their brother George and told him that she thought Daniel's "new girlfriend" was "fast."

Born in New Hampshire, Urban A. Woodbury came to Morristown at the age of two. He graduated from the UVM School of Medicine in 1859, but he never practiced. At the outbreak of the Civil War in 1861, he enlisted in Company H, 2nd Regiment of Vermont Volunteers, and at the Battle of Bull Run, he lost his right arm. Captain Woodbury later gained prominence as owner and proprietor of the Van Ness House. He was elected a city alderman in 1880, mayor in 1884, Vermont lieutenant governor in 1888, and governor in 1894.

Urban A. Woodbury II, grandson of the governor, owned Appletree Point Farms on North Avenue, starting in 1915. His herd of Guernsey cattle was one of the finest in the country and won regional and national championships from 1920 to 1924. Woodbury gave up cattle in 1931 and developed the 225-acre farm into an exclusive summer resort.

Rear Admiral Henry T. Mayo, a Burlington native, was commander in chief of the U.S. Atlantic Fleet during World War I. He was awarded the Distinguished Service Medal, Grand Officer of the Legion of Honor, and received Grand Cordon of the Rising Sun from the Japanese government.

Thomas H. Murphy was born in Burlington in 1860. In 1893, he bought the old Rowe Hotel, on the northwest corner of Church and Cherry Streets, remodeled it, and renamed it the New Sherwood, which he ran successfully till his death in 1917. He also built the World in Motion Theatre, later named the Majestic, on Bank Street. The theater was reduced to a parking lot, and the hotel burned in 1937.

John F. Kidder grew up in Burlington and in 1896 established his plumbing and steam fitting business. He designed and patented over twenty-one tools and machines and after 1902 manufactured them for worldwide sale. Kidder was superintendent of Burlington Water Works for sixteen years. He served two terms as a city alderman.

Valedictorian of the UVM College of Medicine's Class of 1884, Donly C. Hawley practiced medicine in Burlington for many years, also serving as a surgeon at Mary Fletcher, Fanny Allen, and DeGoesbriand Hospitals. Prominent in regional and national medical associations, Dr. Hawley was a Burlington school commissioner (1893–1901), mayor (1901–03), and state senator (1917–19). He died in 1926.

Elbridge S. Adsit, born in Essex County, New York, moved with his family to Burlington in 1867. He joined John J. Bigelow in the coal business as Adsit & Bigelow in 1875, buying out his partner in 1893. In 1907, he laid out the plans and built Adsit Place. Adsit was a city alderman (1897–1901) and was chief of police during the administration of Mayor Woodbury.

Moving from Waterbury in 1868, Henry Wells became a member of the Wells, Richardson & Company partnership. After the firm incorporated in 1883, he was treasurer, vice president, and finally president of the Wells and Richardson Company, which manufactured proprietary medicines and dyes at 125–129 College Street. Wells was a trustee of the Burlington Savings Bank and, after 1890, also a trustee of the Mary Fletcher Hospital.

Harvey D. Yandow returned from service in World War I and established the Yandow Tire and Battery Service Station in April 1921. His partner was his older brother, Harry A. Yandow. The station later expanded to become the Yandow Motor Company, a Pontiac dealership.

Of Scottish ancestry, Henry Todd was born in Lachute, Quebec, in 1868 and came to Burlington when he was twenty-one years old. Todd was a steward of the Home for Destitute Children from 1896 to 1910. He became a deputy sheriff in 1906 under Sheriff James Allen, was made turnkey in 1910, and was elected Chittenden County sheriff in 1918.

Born in Crown Point in 1856, Earl E. Morgan moved to Burlington and was founder and president of Morgan Brothers, manufacturers of doors, window sashes, and blinds. Morgan served two terms as a city alderman. He died in 1926.

John S. Patrick was a native of Hinesburg. From a store clerk in 1875, Patrick rose to become chief executive of several companies: the G.S. Blodgett Company, the Eastern Magnesia Talc Company, the Southern Mineral Corporation, and the Majestic Theatre Company. Patrick was also a director of the Chittenden County Trust Company.

Roy L. Patrick, son of John S., began his career in 1898 as proprietor of the Standard Coal & Ice Company. He merged it with two other firms in 1908 to form the Consolidated Ice Company. Treasurer of the G.S. Blodgett Company after 1916, he became president of the Rock of Ages Corporation in 1925. His home on South Willard Street is now Rowell Hall, a Champlain College dormitory. He is remembered in the naming of UVM's Patrick Gymnasium.

Warren R. Austin graduated from UVM in 1899 and was admitted to the Vermont Bar in 1902. He represented the American International Corporation in China for several years, then set up his law practice in Burlington in 1917. Austin was elected U.S. senator in 1931 to fill the unexpired term of Senator Greene and was reelected in 1934. A framer of the United Nations charter in 1945, Austin served as the first United States ambassador to the U.N. from 1946 to 1953.

Michael C. Dorn was born in Zurich in 1871 and came to Burlington in 1898, where he opened a restaurant in the Strong Block. He sold it in 1915 and opened a restaurant to serve the officers and men at Fort Ethan Allen. Starting in 1917, Dorn also made and marketed Dorn's Venetian Ginger Ale, which became popular all over New England.

George M. Herberg arrived in Burlington in 1903 and was chief clerk of the Champlain Transportation Company until 1920. In that year, he opened the Herberg Auto Service Company, which was located for many years on St. Paul Street.

A native of Dorset, John J. Flynn was an organizer and part owner of the Burlington Traction Company, which provided electric trolley service in the city from 1893 to 1929. The electric power was generated at the Otter Creek Falls by the Vergennes Water Power Company, of which Flynn was also a part owner. He succeeded Elias Lyman as president of the trolley company but then sold its assets in 1929 to William Appleyard's Burlington Rapid Transit Company, which provided more flexible bus service. Starr Farm Beach was Flynn's country estate, and he is remembered in the naming of Flynn Avenue and the Flynn Theater.

Born in 1877 in Granville, New York, Clarence H. Beecher received his medical degree from UVM in 1900. He later studied in Boston, New York, and Vienna. Beecher was an instructor and later professor of medicine at UVM after 1911. He was very active in civic affairs, serving as alderman in 1919–21 and 1923–25. As mayor of Burlington from 1924 to 1929, he oversaw the construction of a new city hall, Memorial Auditorium, Central Fire Station, a new junior high school, the city airport, and of course, the construction of a new Winooski Bridge after the 1927 flood.

Joseph T. Smith graduated from Dartmouth in 1906 and entered the talcum powder business in Rochester, Vermont. When the Eastern Magnesia Talc Company was formed in 1924, Smith became its vice president and general manager of operations. He was also a director of several other Vermont companies.

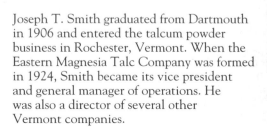

116

A Vergennes native, Robert W. McCuen attended Middlebury College and Boston University Law School. He was elected to the legislature in 1906 and 1910. McCuen served in France during the First World War, advancing to lieutenant colonel. He resumed his law career in Vermont after the war and was appointed collector of Internal Revenue for the District of Vermont by President Harding in 1921.

Oscar Heininger organized the Kieslich Construction Company in 1915 with his son Alfred and Albert V. Kieslich. Over the next forty years, the company built many landmarks in Burlington, among them the original DeGoesbriand Hospital, Burlington Junior High School, the E.B. & A.C. Whiting Company plant, and the Maltex Building. Heininger served the city as superintendent of the Burlington Water Department. He was also a founder of the German Club.

Born in Burlington in 1886, Alfred H. Heininger graduated from Burlington High in 1904 and from UVM in 1908. He received his law degree from Boston University in 1916. Returning to Burlington, he became secretary-treasurer of Kieslich Construction Company, a position he held until 1957. Heininger was a state senator from 1935 to 1941, and from 1935 to 1959, he was the old-age assistance commissioner. Shown here in Montpelier in 1939, he ran as a Democrat for governor in 1936 but lost to George D. Aiken.

Erna (Neumann) Heininger, on the left, attended Tufts Dental School in Boston, where she met Alfred Heininger in 1916 and later married in 1920. She became the first woman dentist in Vermont, opening an office on the corner of Church and College Streets. She is shown here aboard the *Ticonderoga* in 1926 with Mrs. Rehder, a Boston friend.

A generous donor to Fletcher Free Library, Minnie Pickering is remembered in the naming of the Pickering Room, which is used for many community functions.

This 1955 gathering at WDOT was celebrating the station's first anniversary. Among those standing are Jack Barry, Ted Muller, Fred Fayette (fifth from left), Don Bartlett, Val Carter, and John Patrick; seated, from left to right, are Beverly St. Germain, Noe Duchaine, Roger Laroche, unidentified, and Paula Dame.

"Goody" Goodreau, on the right, was the guest on Val Carter's WJOY radio show later in the decade. Goodreau was well known in Burlington as a pianist and organist, and he played regularly at the Holiday Inn.

Eleven

Events

Many retail stores and businesses operated on North Street during the last century. This heavy snowfall during the 1880s may have obliterated signs, but it didn't impede the flow of commerce for very long.

The Hotel Burlington and Walker Block fire attracted many spectators on January 14, 1887. In 1837, Samuel Huntington had opened a bookstore on the corner at the site of the former jail. The hotel was sold in 1839 to T.F. and W.L. Strong, who converted it into a commercial block. After the fire, Huntington relocated his bookstore onto Church Street.

This hose cart, owned by Ethan Allen Engine Company No. 4, was probably among the equipment used to fight the Hotel Burlington fire. The cart was presented to the "Ethans" on September 30, 1874, by the Trojan Hook and Ladder Company No. 3 of Troy, New York.

Lumber yards, warehouses, the Pioneer Shops' incubator space for small manufacturers, and the Central Vermont Railroad Station dominate the waterfront below Battery Park during the 1880s.

The majority of the shops and lumber facilities shown in the previous photograph were destroyed by fire June 6, 1888. The blaze started in a kiln used to dry lumber. The train station was spared. George Wright saved George Linsley's records from destruction.

George D. Sherman conducted the Burlington Military Band. Several of his band scores, including "Salute to Burlington," were used by John Philip Sousa. The band played concerts in Burlington and throughout New England. They are shown at a gathering in Old Orchard Beach, Maine, in 1880. Sherman died at age eighty-three when struck by a car while crossing Park Street at the corner of Sherman.

The Boxer Hose Team is pictured here after winning a firemen's competition during 1914. The photograph was taken on Pitkin Street. Bill Powell (in suit), managed the team. Others are: William Hammond (1), Cathedral High School coach; Louis Lavalley (7), a city alderman; Newton Lavery (8), the fire chief; and John Francis (13), the police chief.

President Coolidge and his wife, Grace, participated in University of Vermont commencement exercises in1928. Grace Goodhue Coolidge was born at 315 St. Paul Street and married Calvin Coolidge at 312 Maple Street. Her father was Andrew Goodhue, whose grave is in the Green Mountain Cemetery.

Colchester Avenue ends abruptly at the Winooski River after the devastating 1927 flood washed out the bridge between Burlington and Winooski. When offered federal assistance, Governor John Weeks refused it and told President Coolidge, "Vermont will take care of its own."

Three electric trolley cars were marooned on the Winooski side when the bridge went out. They continued to service Winooski-Fort Ethan Allen and Essex Junction, taking on foot passengers crossing the temporary pontoon bridge until the new bridge was completed.

Erected under the supervision of an engineering company from Fort Dupont, Delaware, and led by First Lieutenant Leslie Groves, the temporary pontoon bridge is visible on the right. Groves later became a major general and directed the Manhattan Project, which developed the atom bomb.

The first bridge connecting Burlington and Colchester was built around 1846 and named for Dr. Bernard F. Heineberg, purported to be the first person to cross the bridge when called from his Colchester Point farm to deliver a Burlington baby. This 1936 photograph shows the opening of the third bridge to span the river.

Charles Lindbergh inspects the *Spirit of St. Louis* during an unscheduled stop at the Burlington airport. He left for Albany about twenty minutes later. This snapshot was taken by a local resident.

BUNKER HILL COMMUNITY COLLEGE

3 6189 00059 0561

Miss Vermont of 1954, Georgia Lauriso, assists Carlene King Johnson with the sash which proclaims her Miss Vermont of 1955. Val Carter is the master of ceremonies.

3795 2087